# purnell's new book of
# BIKES

Edited by Laurie Caddell

# Introduction

**by Graham Noyce**
1979 world champion and five times British champion

Motorcycle sport has been my hobby since I started riding a bike at the age of six. Maybe six sounds too young, but it gives good experience and helps to build confidence. I did not commence schoolboy scrambling until I was 10.

My first scrambles machine was bought for £5, and never have I had such an unreliable bike! But it provided a whole lot of fun, alongside all the disappointments when it kept breaking down — and many good friends let me borrow their bikes. In those early days, I learned how to lose as well as how to win.

There are so many happy memories from my schoolboy scrambling days, and I cannot recollect one dull moment. Nothing seemed to matter then, but in later years I became a professional scrambler and there is no denying that the responsibility is great. It puts great pressure on a rider, but the atmosphere is fantastic.

Before I was 16, I rode in a few schoolboy trials. I often wished I had tried my luck in grass track racing, too, but I decided that it was scrambling which had the most appeal. Six years of scramble experience was behind me by the time I rode in my first adult race.

Schoolboy motorcycling has come up from almost nothing in recent times, and it provides the groundwork on which many young riders have built their careers during the 1970s. I was lucky to start when I did, and I can thoroughly recommend that every keen schoolboy should get involved in motorcycling.

This book, with its chapters on every different branch of the sport, is something very special — just right for the average schoolboy who is wondering how to get started. Motorcycling is more popular today than at any time before, and I am proud to be part of it.

**Graham Noyce rose from the ranks of schoolboy scrambling events to become the British champion five times and the 1979 World Champion.**

ISBN 0 361 05387 8

Copyright © 1982 Purnell Publishers Limited, Paulton, Bristol BS18 5LQ

Designed and produced for Purnell Books by Autumn Publishing Limited, 10 Eastgate Square, Chichester, Sussex

Revised edition produced by Mallard Publishing, 5 Blandford Road, London W4 1DU

Made and printed in Great Britain by Purnell and Sons (Book Production) Limited, Paulton

# Contents

Photographs
pp 33, 36, 37, 60, 61 Don Morley; pp 48, 49, 52, 53, 73, title
page and endpapers Allsport; pp 14 & 15 STEP Management
Services Ltd; pp 69 & 71 Honda; p 13 Philip Carr; p 42
Nicholls; p 47 Malcolm J Dodd; p 54 Leo Volgelzany; p 70
Suzuki; p 76 G Herringshaw.

# The Early Days

To be a motorcyclist in the pioneering days of the early 1900s called for more than mere bravery. It needed a rather special kind of nuttiness, because the rider was going to be a man on his own, unable to call on help from others should anything go wrong – as it frequently did. The simple reason was that nobody else knew anything about engines either.

The idea of mechanical propulsion was not totally new. After all, steam trains had been chugging about for almost 75 years. But *personal* mechanical propulsion was a different concept, and it was quite likely that a motorcyclist could ride all day without seeing a car or another motorcycle.

Infrequent motor traffic meant that there were no filling stations either. The earliest riders had to order supplies of fuel, in two-gallon cans, direct from the refinery, collecting it themselves from the nearest railway station. But within a few years some chemists and bicycle dealers were beginning to keep a few cans in stock.

Even so, any journey of more than a short distance required careful planning, including sending telegrams to towns along the projected route to be sure that fuel would be available at the right time. Today, it is unlikely that a motorcycle tool kit would contain more than a few spanners, but back in 1903 "The Motor Cycle" (the only journal then covering the subject) advised, in all seriousness, that the tourist should carry a kit containing, as a

minimum, the following:

Two adjustable spanners; A pair of gasfitter's pliers; One screwdriver; One half-round file; A four-volt test lamp; A roll of copper wire; A large oil can, filled with lubricating oil; A small oil can, filled with paraffin; Asbestos washers; Asbestos string; Insulating tape; A tyre repair outfit; A roll of prepared canvas (at least one yard) for repairing a burst outer cover; Square of patching rubber; A large tube of rubber solution; A short length of leather belting; A length of leather thong; A couple of rags, or a piece of cotton waste.

To understand just why all this kit should be necessary, we must look at the roads of the day. They were not tar-covered (indeed, the first experimental stretch of tar-macadam roadway in Britain was just outside Staines, and was laid down in 1903) but consisted of rolled stone topped with a finer layer of grit.

**Above: One of Britain's first mass-produced engines was the JAP, made in North London by John A. Prestwich. This 1903 model has a frame built from Chater-Lea lugs.**

In summer, the speed of a passing vehicle could be judged by the height of its dust cloud above the hedgerow; in winter the road – particularly towards the edges – would be a sea of mud interspersed with water-filled potholes, and its degree of slipperiness would depend upon the local geology, with chalky or limestone areas offering a surface on which it was near impossible for a motorcycle to remain upright for long.

Of course, the motorcycle of the 1900s was not as we know it now. A few foolhardy souls had tried steam propulsion (an American named Lucius Copeland had even fitted a small steam engine to a penny-farthing bicycle), but it was not until the bicycle had become generally acceptable in very much the present form, and Gottfried Daimler had demonstrated the possibilities of the relatively light petrol engine as a propulsion unit, that the two elements came together in the motorised bicycle. At first, nobody was quite sure where the engine should be placed. Raleigh and Royal Enfield tried carrying it on a bracket in front of the steering head. Singer adopted the ingenious Perks and Birch idea of mounting it inside a cast-aluminium-spoked wheel which could be substituted for the front wheel of a tricycle, or the rear wheel of a bicycle. The majority clipped it to the front of the frame front down tube, just ahead of the pedalling gear.

It was left to the two Werner brothers, Russian refugees who had settled in Paris, to produce the first true motorcycle by mounting the engine in the place where the pedals of a pushbike would be. That was in 1902, and although the Werners patented their scheme, it didn't take other makers long to find a way around the patent (usually by building a loop-type frame, with the main tube passing under the engine crankcase). Striking out on a completely different path, Yorkshire engineer Joah Phelon used the engine as part of the frame (it replaced the normal front down tube) and this worked so well that it was employed, at first by Humber and by P & M, and later by Panther, right through to the 1960s.

However, we are getting a little ahead of the story. Almost invariably, the pioneer machine would have neither gearbox nor clutch, but instead a leather or rubber-and-canvas belt would take the drive direct from the engine shaft to a large pulley clipped or spoked to the rear wheel.

Certainly, chain was already known (all bicycles used it by this time) but nobody had yet thought of the shock-absorber, and a direct chain gave a very harsh drive. On the other hand, a nice springy belt would take up the imperfections in the power delivery and provide a smooth ride.

Most of the engines available to the early motorcycle builders

**Below: This motorcycle went to war in 1915. It was made by Matchless of London for the Motor Machine Gun Corps. Most machine-gun sidecars used were made by Scott or Clyno. Thousands of motorcycles were used during the two world wars.**

were of continental origin (Minerva from Belgium, De Dion from France, and so on) mainly because Britain's ruling classes of the time were extremely horse-minded and did what they could to stifle progress towards a mechanised society. The law that a man with a red flag had to walk in front of a self-propelled vehicle had been scrapped in 1896, but even so there was an overall national speed limit of only 19 km/h (12 mph) – and less than that in some towns.

Early engines were very low-powered, and in most cases pedalling gear was retained because the rider needed it to help his machine to climb a hill. As one pioneer rider described

it, "You waited until the road was clear; made a furious rush at the hill on full throttle; pedalled like mad as the engine revs dropped; hopped off and ran alongside when the engine showed signs of dying on you; and eventually pushed the last bit, unless some side lane furnished the chance of a second power rush."

There were plenty of snags. For one thing, when the engine was running the bicycle's freewheel on the rear hub was working overtime. In due course it would overheat and seize up, and the pedals would then start flying round like a circular saw, the rider having to raise his legs to avoid injury. That was why the oil can full of

Above: Messrs W.J.M. Sproule, P. Shaw and W.C. Drake astride their gleaming motorcycles at Carlisle Drill Hall for the start of the 1913 International Six-Days Trial. Sproule and Drake won gold medals, Shaw a silver.

paraffin was needed, to be squirted into the freewheel until it un-seized and was operative again!

Motorcycles were tall and top-heavy, and if an uphill bend had to be tackled on a wet day, the chances were that they would skid wildly and lie down! That usually resulted in a bent pedal, and hence the larger of the two recommended adjustable spanners was needed to

10

bend it straight again.

Gradually the motorcycle was making headway, but two circumstances in particular were to hasten its progress. The first of these was the introduction, in 1907, of the Isle of Man TT Races; the second was the outbreak of World War One. The races, with their healthy competition between factories, inspired the rapid development of frame, engine and transmission design. Wartime conditions saw many thousands of motorcycles in use at the battlefront, and as the science of metallurgy grew, so the army machines became ever more reliable.

When peace returned in 1918, the motorcycle was ready to face the future; but it was already a very different machine from that which the pioneer rider had known. The spadework of overall development had been done, what was left for the future was refinement.

**Below: Percy Bischof and his passenger Beatrice Langston in a Triumph combination in the 1912 Scottish Six-Days Trial.**

# Buying Your First Bike

Now that learner riders are restricted to machines of 12 bhp/125cc or less, one would assume that the choice of machine available would be limited. But because the "learner" market is a very lucrative one, the main manufacturers are making sure that there is ample choice for the prospective customer.

So how do you go about singling out that machine which will be ideal for you? Obviously, price is of prime importance, but if your pocket can stand the cost of a new machine, which of the comparably priced bikes is best? First, work out what you want from your bike when you use it regularly. Do you need an economical commuter machine which is light and easy to handle in traffic, or do you want a sporty job for recreation which has the best performance available and good looks to match?

If it is the former, then you should be looking for a four-stroke-engined bike. Put simply, although a four-stroke is more complicated in design than a two-stroke, it will generally be more economical, easier to ride and need less maintenance. Ridden gently, a good 125cc four-stroke should return almost 100 mpg, yet still have a top speed of more than 60 mph.

On the other hand, the two-stroke engine will feel more eager to the rider and produce that extra push in acceleration. Although generally needing more attention than a four-stroker, the two-stroke motor is easier to work on, having no valve gear to dismantle when stripping the engine.

Two-strokes need frequent decoking of the cylinders, but this is a simple task which a practised hand should accomplish without any trouble. A good two-stroke will top out at 70 mph or just over and return up to 85 mpg. However, it will not give you anything like that if you use its extra top speed and acceleration capabilities.

There are three basic styles of bike to choose from: the conventional roadster, the trail/off-road type and the American-style customs. Apart from being attracted by their respective looks and your obvious preferences, each type has its own particular riding characteristics.

The roadster will be a little heavier to steer around town than the others, but its slightly lean-forward riding style will make for less tiring journeys at higher speeds. The trail bike will generally be taller than the others and maybe even lighter, and its more vertical steering angle will be helpful threading in and out of traffic; of course, it will also be handy off road too.

Finally, the custom versions offered have lower seats than the others so are particularly suited to the smaller rider. The higher bars will give a more upright riding position which again makes for easier town work. However, this will work against the rider at higher speeds because he will offer a larger area to the wind which will be tiring, and a strain on the arm and neck muscles.

The Japanese manufacturers have the widest range of machine to choose from, but if buying one of the cheaper European machines, check out spares prices and availability because a breakdown away from home and your local

dealer could be costly. Work out what *you* want from a bike and then look at all the brochures to find one which fits your needs.

Of course, if you can't stretch to the price of a 125cc but still need a proper bike, it is worth checking out the 80cc and 100cc classes, where for less money you can find bikes which perform as well as the 125cc machines and, with their lighter weight, will be even easier to manage.

The golden rule is deciding on what you want and not what friends or dealers might try to convince you that you think you want.

**The moment when you buy your first bike is an unforgettable time. Make sure that you are buying what you want – do not let the dealer persuade you into purchasing a bike which you are not sure about.**

# Bike Clubs

You can learn a great deal about motor bikes by reading books but the best way of gaining full appreciation of your bike is to join a club. There are several advantages. Perhaps the most important one is that they are open to riders of all levels. This means that if you have been learning to ride for only a couple of weeks, or are fully experienced and equally at home on moto-cross or road bike, you will still get plenty of benefits from joining a club.

Bike riders generally like to travel in company. This may be by having a pillion passenger or travelling in convoy with other riders. Most people have heard of the notorious Hells Angels, but whatever the reputation they have acquired, they are first and foremost a bike club, and it was the enjoyment of bikes which first brought them together.

There are hundreds of clubs all over Britain, ranging from casual groups of friends who meet perhaps once a month in a local pub to discuss bikes, to properly ordered societies relating to one particular bike, like the Triumph or Norton Owners' Clubs. The things which they all have in common are a love of bikes and the fact that they are under the Auto Cycle Union, which controls all motor cycle riding in this country. This means that the ACU sets rules for trials' riding or road racing and both sections have clubs of enthusiasts too.

Membership of a club is

**Below: The best way to learn is from a trained instructor. Here a group of pupils are learning about changing gear.**

very inexpensive and a good one will give tremendous benefits for the subscription paid. One of the most popular activities is the open evening, where a guest speaker from the police, fire or ambulance service will give a short talk and answer questions. Equally popular are talks by leading riders or experts from particular makers explaining technical points about the bikes.

This, however, is far from the only activity. Most ordinary clubs will hold weekend runs, perhaps to the sea or to the countryside and places of interest. These runs serve several purposes. They teach the less experienced riders how to ride in convoy, showing them that bikes should never travel in groups of more than five together. They teach road sense, with the more experienced riders advising others. They enable you to travel with a group of riders with similar interests to yourself, and help you to make many new friends. And they are extremely useful if something goes wrong with your bike.

Of course no rider ever looks forward to a break-down but it can happen. Unless you are an experienced mechanic, breaking down on an open road can be a frustrating, expensive and time-consuming experience. If this happens when you are on a run with the club, you can be sure that the rest of the group will rally round and help you. In all but a very few cases, between them they will be able to get your bike running again.

As you become more experienced, you may like to join club members on a holiday abroad. Many clubs now travel

to the Continent, camping on the excellent sites available and visiting sometimes several countries on one trip.

The clubs have several other activities such as competitions and quizzes, but often the meetings will do no more than provide a place for bike riders to meet together and chat about problems or the latest topics of interest in the bike world.

Of course they will also give you a great deal of help in learning about maintenance, because every good bike rider will learn quickly how to do all his basic maintenance and will probably soon be able to handle all but major jobs.

Clubs often give an opportunity to buy spare parts at a discount, which can be very useful if you have an older model of bike.

**Above: It is best to learn to control your bike fully before venturing out on to the road.**

There are so many advantages to being a member of a bike club that it is surprising to know that there are still riders who do not belong to one. They do not know what they are missing.!

To find out the address of your nearest club, get in touch with your local motor cycle shop, which will usually be able to give details. If you want to join a specialist club, get in touch with the manufacturers, who are keen to encourage people to join such organisations.

15

# Maintaining Your Machine

No special skills are needed for routine maintenance of your motorcycle, only common sense, and regular safety checks should ensure that potential trouble areas are spotted long before they become expensive repair jobs. Getting into the habit of checking the bike before riding may seem to be something of a tedious task but in the long run it will be worth it.

Always make sure that tyres and valves are in good condition and that the bike is running with the manufacturers' recommended tyre pressures. Variations here can upset a machine's handling, making it difficult to ride and dangerous.

The next obvious step is to make sure that the chain is correctly tensioned and lubricated. Halfway between the rear-wheel sprocket and the gearbox, lift the chain towards the swing arm; about 20 mm is the correct amount of slack. Any difference either way will cause adverse wear on the chain, with worn bearings the result of a too-tight chain.

At the lower end of the machine, make sure that there is plenty of material left on the brake pads (on disc brake machines). It is usual for manufacturers to have warning lines on the pads so that you can see exactly how much there is left. If the pads are left until the metal shows through, it will mean the discs themselves will be scored and need replacing. If your bike has spoked wheels, a light tap on each spoke with a screwdriver should give a faint

"ring", signifying that it is correctly tensioned, although it is possible to feel just how taut they are by pressing them gently. If they are loose, be careful when tightening them because they can puncture the inner tube.

Cast wheels should be cleaned and checked for cracking, which can often be the result of mounting kerbs too quickly. If there is a flaw, this will get worse the next time the wheel is put under load and the consequences are obvious.

The wheel bearings can be checked by pushing and pulling the wheel and feeling for slight movement. This is easily accomplished by putting the bike on its centre stand with either wheel hanging over the edge of the kerb in turn.

Apart from checking the general area of the engine for leaks and seepages, a lot can be learned of engine condition by regular checking of the sparking plugs. A healthy plug will look slightly brown in colour with no obvious signs of wear. If the plug is matt black, then the fuel mixture is too rich. (Increased fuel consumption is another obvious sign of this condition.) If the plug is grey in appearance, this will mean that the mixture is too weak and that the plug is overheating. Run too long like this and the sparking plug will start to break up.

If the plug is black and shiny, it means that there is oil getting into the combustion chambers. On a two-stroke it means that the oil pump is wrongly calibra-

ted, while on a four-stroke it means that there is a serious problem. Either valve guides are worn or the cylinder rings and bores. Obviously, the plugs need not be checked every time the bike is fired up, but the more regular the checks, the more chance there is of finding a problem before it gets too bad.

A quick glimpse at the inside of the exhaust pipes is a simple way to check up on the engine. Again, black sooty deposits mean too rich and grey/white deposits mean too weak.

The rest of the simple checks involve making sure that all bolts and nuts are tight (but don't overtighten them) and that all electrical connections are free from corrosion. A light jelly on the battery terminals will protect them during the winter.

One major task which can be carried out quite quickly and easily is decoking a small two-stroke engine. Two-strokes are very dirty engines and soon build up a fair amount of carbon in the combustion chambers and exhaust ports. If the motor gets badly encrusted with the carbon, performance will suffer and fuel consumption will rise dramatically.

It is not necessary to decoke the motor every other week as some people will tell you. In fact, for older engines a light build-up of the black substance on the outer edge of the piston and at the top of the bore can work as an extra oil seal.

A simple decoke is carried out as follows. First, remove

16

the exhaust pipe from the cylinder; if this is difficult to remove after the bolts have been undone, gentle tapping with a rubber mallet should free it. Again, if the head is still firmly attached to the barrel after the securing studs are unbolted, a mallet again should be used, taking care to tap each corner in turn so that the head isn't knocked out of shape.

Once the head is removed, use the kick start to get the piston to the top of its stroke and scrape away the carbon. Make sure that you use something with a blunt edge otherwise you will gouge the piston itself. When most of the larger lumps of deposits have come away, use wire wool to get the rest off. Finally, the last remains should be removed with a very fine wet-or-dry paper. It can help to use a light covering of metal polish on the paper but if you do this it must be removed afterwards. Paraffin is a handy solvent to take away the polish film.

The next stage is to apply grease to the top of the piston and then move it down to the bottom of its stroke and apply more grease to the cylinder walls. When the exhaust port is uncovered, you will probably find that it has its share of build-up in the corners. Being careful not to gouge the metal, chip away the offending particles and sweep them gently out with a soft brush.

Don't worry about a few particles of carbon falling back into the cylinder; these will stick to the grease-lined cylinder and can be removed by bringing the piston back up to the top slowly. The piston will bring up a wave of carbon-

enriched grease which can be wiped off.

Be careful when dealing with the cylinder head because it is very easy to damage the threads around the sparking-plug hole. Patience is essential because it is best to use a large needle to clear out the threads themselves. Follow the same procedure as with the piston and bores by finishing off with wet-or-dry paper and polish, again using a solvent to remove afterwards.

While the engine is apart, it is best to check the piston rings to make sure they are still in order, and look at the cylinder bore for signs of wear. If there is any slight scoring, it is best to effect a remedy before things go too far.

Before putting the exhaust system back, pull out the exhaust tailpipe from the silencer and clean it well. If it is particularly fouled it may be best to get a new one. Remember that clogged exhaustways can seriously affect fuel consumption on a two-stroke, and

**Above: A young rider adjusts the tickover on his Honda MB-5.**

with petrol being so expensive, it can be false economy not to be ruthless when deciding what has to go.

When reassembling the engine, take care to tighten down the head bolts in the correct order and to the right torque settings, and make sure that new gaskets are fitted where required. Once a gasket has been disturbed, it is usually best to replace because they never refit with the snugness of new items.

Once the procedure has been tried, it should be possible to carry it out again in under an hour with a single-cylinder bike and not much longer if it is a twin.

The golden rule is that the more time you spend checking your bike before things go wrong will mean less time standing next to it late at night, miles from nowhere, wondering why it broke down "out of the blue"

# Young Competition

There have been motorcycle scrambles since 1924, but not until 1964 was it possible for schoolboys to take an active part in this branch of the sport.

Throughout those 40 years, the youngsters had to content themselves with watching from the sidelines – longing for the day when they were old enough to compete.

But now all that has changed. It was 15 years ago that the world's first schoolboy scramble was held – near Reading, in Berkshire. And it attracted just three competitors!

Today, thousands of lads between the ages of six and 16 are riding in schoolboy motocross every weekend throughout the summer. And, since 1967, schoolboy grass track racing has flourished, too. But it is motocross which has gained most ground.

Inevitably, it has been the cradle of brilliant riders. Graham Noyce, for instance, spent six years in schoolboy scrambling before he launched out into adult sport at the age of 16 – and he has taken the British Championship title five times.

Much the same sort of thing has been happening where motorcycle trials are concerned – though the first schoolboy trial dates back to 1924. But in the early days the events were held on public roads and were therefore restricted to boys old enough to hold a driving licence.

Then, in 1972, the first schoolboy trials club was formed – and this branch of the

**Above: Former National Junior Trials Champion Graham Birkett takes the plunge on his Yamaha.**

**Above, right: Astride a Z4 Techomoto, Jason Rimmell shows the skill that won him factory sponsorship at the age of 8.**

**Right: They're off! It's the start of the action-packed cadets' race at Bydean Farm in Hampshire.**

sport proved an immediate success. Nowadays there are trials clubs in all part of Great Britain – not so numerous as for motocross and grass track racing, but with every bit as much enthusiasm.

Speed plays no part in motorcycle trials, so the risk of injury is minimal. Almost equally rare is machine damage. In consequence the cost of competing is lower – and every schoolboy who yearns to take part in motorcycle sport should spend at least 12 months as a trials rider before trying

his hand at something more ambitious.

However, there is not the slightest doubt that trials do provide a good stepping-stone for motocross or grass track races, and parents should bear this in mind when making plans for their sons to compete.

Unfortunately, the cost of machinery has risen to astronomical proportions. In its early days, schoolboy motorcycling was a very inexpensive sport. For trials, motocross and grass tracks, 125cc BSA Bantams were the almost automatic choice – reliable little bikes which could be bought for around £10.

Now all that has changed. A really top-class foreign 125cc motocross machine can cost more than £1,000 with all the trimmings. You may wonder how many youngsters have parents who are prepared to spend that sort of money.

But the answer is quite a lot, because many lads are given new motorcycles with which to start schoolboy motocross. This can of course affect their sense of values if they have first-class machines from the start.

In many ways the old-fashioned approach is better. Getting started on a modest level, learning to ride a cheap second-hand bike, and if mechanical trouble crops up, then repairing the machine will develop a knowledge of engines which can be very useful in later years.

Another invaluable branch of schoolboy motor cycling is the trick-riding display teams which several clubs have formed. These performed in public – usually in aid of

**Above: John Taylor on a 250cc Montesa during a charity show. John helped to form the Waltham Chase Display Team.**

**Right: The youngsters in this race are all under 10, but they are in total control of their machines.**

charity – and help to demonstrate the youngsters' skill to a wide audience.

Members of motorcycle display teams, such as the Imps must have a good sense of balance and machine control. They spend many hours practising, and their ability is quite remarkable.

But not every display team member is an Eddie Kidd in the making! At 18 years of age, dare-devil Eddie became the world's motorcycle long-jump champion. 60 metres (200 ft) leaps were nothing special to Eddie when he had perfected his act, and sailing high over a

line of double-decker buses became commonplace.

There will be thousands of youngsters reading this book who have never seen any form of schoolboy motorcycle sport and who do not know how best to get involved. The first move

must be to discuss the possibility with their parents.

Many adult motorcycle clubs nowadays have youth sections, and they will be pleased to provide information. Membership is not costly, but little purpose is served by joining a local club if it does not have a youth section.

There are schoolboy motorcycle clubs in all parts of the country, and a list of these (with names and addresses of their secretaries) can be obtained from the Auto-Cycle Union, Youth Division, 52 Princes Street, Manchester. But on no account should any money be spent on the purchase of expensive machinery until a schoolboy event has been seen and the requirements properly assessed. Enthusiasm without knowledge can lead to disappointment and disaster!

The schoolboy scene is well established now, and was described recently by Lord Montagu as the most significant happening in post-war motorcycle sport. "Its progress has been nothing less than an explosion," he said.

**Former schoolboy sidecar champions Andy House and passenger Duncan Long. Sidecar scrambling can provide all the thrills and it means that you can share the costs with a friend.**

# Scrambling

**Up! Up! And away goes Brad Lackey – one of the world's most spectacular riders.**

Scrambling is about the toughest form of motorcycle sport. In fact studies on top athletes have shown that it's one of the toughest of all sports when it comes to stamina and physical fitness. Put that together with a large helping of speed and skill, and you've got a recipe for one of the most exciting and exhilarating spectacles on two wheels.

Scrambling, or motocross as it's now often called, has been with us since the 1920s, but it has obviously come a long way since its early beginnings. Then, gentlemen in cloth caps and plus-fours would attempt to pilot their un-wieldy, overweight and underpowered road machines along cross-country tracks and hill climbs. But the principle has remained the same: a reasonably long circuit with a variety of hazards, all to be tackled at the greatest possible speed.

In the beginning, however, the length of the lap was so great, and the machines so un-suitable, that it was more a question of persever-ance and endurance on the part of the strug-gling riders. Something of that still remains.

Motocross will always make big demands on strength and stamina; but with the racing bikes becoming more specialised, not just faster, but lighter and easier to ride, the speed and the skill have become more important.

Because the bikes are that much easier to ride over rough ground, scrambling as a sport has been made possible for people who don't happen to be big muscle-bound Tarzans. Even youngsters of five or six can handle specially-prepared motocross machines, and there is now a great following for the sport in schoolboy racing for boys and girls under 16 years of age. It doesn't mean that motocross tracks have become any easier. If anything, they are a lot harder, because present day bikes can cope with things that would have the old timers floundering.

As the bikes are that much better, the people who organise the races have had to make the tracks harder to keep the element of challenge

**It's the first lap battle with a tightly bunched pack fighting for that first bend.**

25

in the sport. It is that challenge that motocross is all about – man and machine versus all that the terrain can put up against him. The average motocross track is between 1.6 and 3.2 kilometres (1–2 miles) long, but that length may be all contained within a space not much bigger than a farmer's field. It will twist and snake around using all the natural features of the land, especially any hills, ledges or ditches. The important thing is that it isn't flat. Even the straights will have bumps and ruts that can catch the rider out.

The track must also be wide enough to allow a number of bikes side by side, so that there can be overtaking at any part of the course.

The starting line is always the widest part, because there can be over 30 bikes in a line at one time, and one of the most spectacular sights is always the mass charge towards the first corner.

Along the length of the track, which is lined by ropes or wooden fencing, there will be flag marshals and first aid attendants to help in the event of an accident, but although motocross riders tend to fall off a lot, serious injuries are few. Motocross is no more dangerous than sports like rugby or football which probably have a higher rate of broken legs and arms. Part of the reason is that the rider takes care to dress himself in protective gear, like an American football ace. Apart from a proper crash helmet, goggles, gloves and strong boots, he also has tough pants with knee pads and hip pads, and there's plastic armour he can wear to protect his chest, shoulders and elbows. All these not only save skin burns if he slides along hard ground, but also fend off stones and small rocks that can be thrown up by the spinning back wheels of machines in front.

Speeds in motocross are not as high as in road racing because the bikes are geared and tuned for acceleration and pulling power. Although they are capable of anything between 128 and 160 km/h (80–100 mph) depending on size, they are rarely ridden flat-out in top gear because of the tight, twisting tracks. The average lap speed at a motocross is only around 48 km/h (30 mph), but it's not speed down the

**Hidden protection includes knee and hip pad . . .**

**A spectacular mass start is one of the most exciting moments for spectator and competitor.**

26

**then armour for chest, shoulders and shins . . .**   **finally, the complete cover-up.**

**Right:** West German rider Herbert Schmitz makes full use of the banking.

**Below:** Five times 500cc moto-cross World Champion Roger de Coster in action.

**Far right:** Winning team-work, Nick Thompson and his passenger Gary Withers, one of the most successful combinations in British sidecar scrambling.

straights that counts so much as speed through the slow, difficult bits. That's where the skill of the top riders counts. They need a good sense of balance, keen reactions, and a good deal of skill and courage to hurl over 90 kilos (200 lbs) of machine over sheer jumps and up steep hills that would be difficult to scale on foot. And many people would say that the top motocross rider is by far the best all-round motorcycle racer for the combination of skills he needs.

The majority of motocross bikes today use powerful single-cylinder two-stroke engines, with five or six speeds in the gearbox for acceleration. The engines have to be light to keep the weight of the bike down, because although the rest of the frame and wheels are generally lighter than most normal motor-cycles, they can't be too light because they also have to be strong enough to put up with the constant pounding they take round the track.

Most of the development on these bikes has gone into trying to soak up the bumps and jumps so the rider can travel faster over them. As a result, motocross bikes are very high off the ground – so much so that the rider's feet may have difficulty reaching the ground – at rest. Both the front and the back wheel may now move more than a foot up and down independently, which is why the mudguards and seat are always so very high.

The development is as fast as the racing itself. Just as they tune the engines for more power, the people who build motocross bikes have to come up with new ideas every season for the frames and suspension to stay with the opposition. Every year, they have to have a new model to stay on top, but usually, in any one season, someone has that slight racing edge.

There are many factories building motocross bikes for the ordinary rider, not just the big names from Japan like Suzuki, Yamaha and Honda, but a number of European firms like Maico, Husqvarna, KTM, Montesa and Bultaco. From West Germany, Maico have been one of the most popular bikes in Britain during recent years. They were the bike of British Champion Graham Noyce before he was offered a lucrative contract with Honda. Since signing, he increased his tally of British titles to five, and even added the sport's blue riband event, the 500cc World Championship. For him, and for a handful of aces like him,

motocross is not just a sport, but a well-paid living giving him the chance to ride all over Europe and America.

Sidecar-cross is rather a different sport from solo moto-cross, even though they are held on the same tracks and usually at the same meetings. The machines are as different to the solos as sidecar road racers are to 500cc GP bikes, with as much of a difference in riding techniques too.

Powerful four-stroke engines are still favourite with sidecar-cross machines because they are easier to tune for mid-range power than a comparable two stroke. Whereas solo machines are ridden high up the power band for most of the time, the extra weight of the sidecar outfits mean that they travel very much slower so that motors need to accelerate from

almost walking pace on some gradients.

The most popular engine in the last decade has been tuned versions of the twin-cylinder 850cc Norton Commando, while Yamaha's 750cc twin-cylinder four-stroke has recently made its mark. The twin-cylinders' inherent low-speed pull has meant that even tuned four-stroke multis like the Kawasaki 1000 and the six-cylinder Honda CBX motor can't compete with the twins.

The sidecar itself is little more than a lightweight platform used as a base for the acrobatic antics of the passenger, who has a mighty task making sure that the outfit gets enough grip and doesn't overturn. Grab handles are positioned all over the outfit so that the passenger can lean either side for the best effect.

**Above: Motocross star Dave Thorpe, a former schoolboy champion on his works Kawasaki.**

Most sidecars use leading-link forks and complex front suspensions which help to make the steering lighter and more effective and less prone to flapping about, should the rider ease his grip.

Sidecar-cross competitors are a hardy bunch for, although you have to be brave to launch a solo 500cc weighing 220 lb 15 feet into the air at 70 mph, it takes a whole lot more guts to do it with more than 500 lb of sidecar, and something else again to sit next to someone doing it for you!

31

# Sprinting and Drag Racing

In drag racing and sprinting there is room for every kind of motorcycle, from the 50cc in the Junior Class right up to monster machines with two or even three engines. For all of them, there is only one aim – to reach the finishing line in the shortest possible time.

Sprinting is one of the oldest established sports for motorcycles, with events taking place back in the early 1900s on public roads and on the drives of large country houses. The machines of today are not for use on the road however. They need a special smooth track, like an airfield runway. Riders are timed by electronic equipment and the fastest man in a class is the winner of the trophy. There are classes from 50cc through to 3500cc, and also classes for sidecars and for normal road machines.

In 1978 the National Sprint Association introduced a Junior Class in sprinting, with a 50cc limit for machines. It is an ideal chance for young mechanics to design and build their own frames and then try their hands at engine tuning. The motor

**Above: In drag and sprints every second counts. The rider's streamlined position presents the least possible wind resistance.**

from any moped or commuter bike is usable and the class is attracting a number of keen riders who have the chance to ride on racetracks all over the country. Junior sprinting is the only branch of under-16s sport where a schoolboy can ride in full competition on tarmac.

From the early sprints developed drag racing – a new and

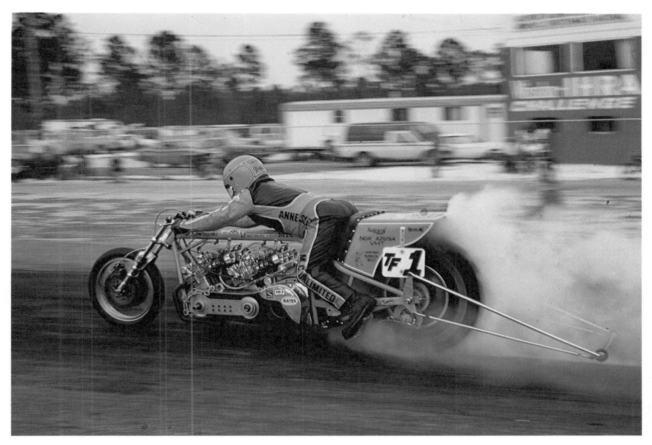

Above: Two engines in one give this streamlined drag-racing bike its awesome power.
Below: John Hobbs on his Weslake Hobbit does a "burn out".
Right: Too much power causes an unintentional "wheelie" by Ian Messenger on his Norton Pegasus.

exciting sport that has produced some of the world's most incredible motorcycles. Starting in America but spreading all over the world, drag racing draws huge crowds to watch two machines race down the 400-metre course. Some events are held on airfield runways, and other are organised on specially built tracks. The best known track in England is Santa Pod Raceway in Bedfordshire, where some of the best riders in the world have competed.

In drag racing, riders start when the starting "traffic light" changes to green. If one of the riders leaves too early, a red light shines and he is eliminated. Reactions must be razor-sharp and the machine control perfect if he is to be first away and get the maximum power all the way down the course.

In both sprinting and drag racing, the start is all-important. For maximum grip on the tarmac surface, the rear tyre is wide and has no tread; it is not rounded at the corners like a racing tyre, but is completely flat. It gives best grip when it is warm, and this is why riders often spin (burn out) the rear tyre in a cloud of blue rubber smoke at the start. With the rear "slick" tyre warm and sticky, there is more grip and this means that more power can be used. With a cold tyre, the enormous power of the engines often spins the rear wheel for 180 metres or more.

Two of the leading lights in British drag racing in the past few years have been John Hobbs and Brian Chapman. Their paths to success were very different.

John Hobbs used two 850cc

Weslake racing engines working together in one machine which is spectacular even to look at. Each engine had a mixture of methanol alcohol and explosive nitro-methane pumped in by a supercharger, and they were linked together by specially made gears. The gearbox and clutch were bought in America and the rear tyre measures 25 cm across. The bike was massive in every way and its great power took John to a best time over the measured distance of 8.15 seconds and a speed of 283 km/h (176 mph) from a standing start.

Brian Chapman used a humble 500cc Vincent engine, made in 1952 and using a number of parts that Brian made himself – racing spares for such an old engine are very hard to find, even if they ever existed! The bike is tiny, only knee-high, with a supercharger that is an old aircraft pump adapted to its new job. The best time for this lightweight combination of man and machine was 8.85 seconds and the top speed 248 km/h (154 mph) – not bad for an engine which was well over a quarter of a century old!

The competitor who rules European drag racing is the Dutch ace, Henk Vink. From Amsterdam, Henk is the man who has guided his four-cylinder Kawasaki to the first sub 8-second time in Europe, with a finishing speed of close to 200 mph. Henk has professional mechanics to keep his fleet of racing machines in good order – he has the choice of three bikes when he sets out for a race meeting and keeps yet another bike, with two

Kawasaki engines, for special demonstrations.

Henk Vink is also a world sprint record holder. In 1977 the brave Dutchman wrestled his bike over a measured kilometre in a time of 16.09 seconds, with a finishing speed of 335 km/h (208 mph). It was a performance that bettered the times of all other vehicles, both cars and motorcycles.

In America there are motor-

cycles bigger than anywhere else in the world: bikes like the Russ Collins's Honda. Using three four-cylinder engines and with a total capacity of 3300cc, it was eventually totally wrecked in a crash. Another monster is the double Harley Davidson of veteran rider Joe Smith, with 3500cc of powerful engines. Several others have built machines with two Harley Davidson engines, but none of them has been as successful as the 1620cc double Norton of Tom Christenson. Racing against machines twice the size of his own, Christenson regularly defeated the huge Harleys, and so christened his British-powered mount "Hogslayer".

In other countries, drag racing is growing. South Africa boasts a Chevrolet car-engined bike that races double-engined Hondas at the Johannesburg

**Tom Christenson spins the rear tyre of his superb 1,620cc double-Norton in a "burn out".**

drag strip. In Australia, English-born Pete Allen has a Kawasaki four-cylinder creation that rules the roost; and in Sweden, Bjorn Knutsson rides a 750cc Triumph and is seldom beaten.

# Grasstrack

Grass track racing probably has more teenage stars than any other branch of motorcycle sport. Thanks to a busy schoolboy section, which caters for boys – and girls – from six years old upwards, each season sees a fresh and talented group moving up to challenge the senior aces.

You have to be 16 to compete in the adult classes; but up to 10 years' previous experience puts a wise head on young shoulders. What chance would the legendary Austin Cresswell, winner of five British titles between 1952 and 1960, have in the sport today? Austin didn't start racing until he was 29!

Some gifted youngsters go straight into the bigger world of speedway but many feel that experience gained on grass can be a great help later on. World speedway ace Peter Collins is a classic example. Peter was a shy and spindly 16-year-old when he first entered grass track, but he had started riding bikes when he was eight and at seventeen won his first British championship. He got another one the next year, too.

Peter is still one of the world's finest speedway riders, but he has never forgotten how to ride grass and there are few better. Yet he can be beaten, just the way he defeated the stars of his youth. Ex-schoolboy grasser Simon Wigg had been dreaming of toppling a world champion in a race since he was eight years old. In 1978, at 17 and in his second season of senior racing, he came from behind to take Collins on the last bend. What a moment! What a dream come true!

Names are being made rapidly in grass track today. Unknown youngsters pop up all the time to score shock wins against the best Britain has to offer.

Grass track has changed dramatically since the first beginnings almost 60 years ago. Those pioneers on their barely modified, road-going Matchless, BSA, Royal Enfield, Norton and Ariel machines could never have imagined how specialised it would eventually become.

The first important engine to emerge was the famous JAP, a single-cylinder racing power-house which completed 50 years' service in 1980. The first one barked round Stamford Bridge speedway track in 1930. It heralded a new era, and yet you will find few differences between that prototype and the more modern version.

The JAP provided ideal power for short, flat-track racing. It produced over 45 bhp in standard form and was flexible enough to accelerate quickly from very low revs. Soon it was dominating speedway and grass track racing, but no one can keep a good idea to themselves for ever.

Czechoslovakia introduced the 500cc Jawa (Eso) engine to challenge the long-serving British motor. It was really just a tidied-up version of the JAP, but it revved higher and

**Right: US gold medal winner Jack Penton during an international six-day enduro, where testing events include trials riding, motocross and time trials.**
**Below: The late Gaylon Mosier, who died in a car crash last year, shows the style which made him 250cc champion in the US.**

produced a little more power. Speedway was soon to become Jawa territory, but the Czech intrusion was not so readily accepted by grass men because the new motor sacrificed some flexibility for top speed and only suited those who could keep an engine buzzing through the turns.

Both engines were in for a nasty shock. The age of the Weslake four-valve cylinder head was just around the corner.

Now it is the mainstay of grass and speedway, though Jawa and then JAP countered with their own four-valve versions. The reason for success is that the Weslake combines the best qualities of both the Jawa and JAP original engines – greater power (around 58 bhp) with flexibility.

Of course other types of engines are used in solo grass track racing. The smallest class, for 250cc machines, is controlled by two-strokes

such as Bultaco, Montesa and Maico, and a good two-stroke 250cc machine is very competitive in the 350cc class against ageing JAPs.

Frame design formed the other major breakthrough when the "speedway diamond" appeared in the 1950s. This formed the basic pattern right up to the present day though there is a trend towards monocoque or box-like construction for the rear sub-frame.

As machines improve, so the speeds increase. Up to 160 km/h (100 mph) is recorded on the larger tracks and the absolute lap record for any grass circuit stands at over 130 km/h (81 mph). Remember that is an average speed and set at international level where no brakes are used.

**Right: Skidding for a fall, but Graham Hurry keeps control of his 350cc Weslake Godden.**

**Left: Ideal conditions as Don Godden on his Weslake Godden 500cc overtakes Phil Crump.**

**Below: Simon Wigg's dream came true when he beat world ace Peter Collins.**

Britain has the largest number of grass track riders anywhere in the world, but the top men go regularly to countries like Germany, France and Holland for higher prize money. Someone like West German idol Egon Muller can command high appearance money because crowds are much larger. Germany, for example, promotes almost 40 international grass and long track events a year.

No one races sidecars on grass quite like the British. From humble beginnings, the British grass track sidecar outfit has developed into a highly sophisticated piece of machinery.

Engines up to 1,000cc are permitted and this brings in the superbike motors of Kawasaki, Honda, Suzuki, Yamaha and that other formidable Weslake, the eight-valve 850cc twin. Engines up to 650cc can be supercharged, though today they are not really competitive.

In Britain big capacity sidecars race clockwise, the opposite way to solos, but there is a 500cc class which goes anti-clockwise, the direction in which the rest of Europe races its "chairs".

It is the big ones that appeal to British fans. They rasp and snort on alcohol fuels, often developing far more power than can ever be transmitted to the ground in forward move-

Above right: Steve Smith and partner Trevor Pye, former British sidecar grass track champions
Above: Rob Shepherd competing in a Scottish Six-days Trial. Right: British trials stalwart Martin Lampkin. Far right: The great speedway rider Peter Collins in action on grass.
Centre: Sergei Tarabanko of Russia who won the world champion on ice speedway title three times, shows the special skills needed for this branch of the sport. The wheels have spikes on them to grip the snow and ice.

**Top left: Mud flies as Simon Wigg holds off Brian Webb and John Butcher in this top-flight grasstrack meeting.**

**Top right: Mark Wadsworth spins into a fast grass track turn at a Shepton Mallet meeting.**

**Left: Les Collins and the 1978 European Champion, Chris Baybutt (271), fight it out.**

**Above: Rob Stoneman and Rowland Broomfield show why understanding is vital in grass track "charioteering".**

ment. Yet they lap not much slower than 500cc solos and demand a high degree of understanding between driver and passenger.

When Britain's best riders clash on a fast track, it is like going back to the spectacle of do-or-die chariot racing in Rome's arenas. If 10 top crews start in one race, it's a safe bet that at least five will arrive at the first turn together.

That's where races can be won or lost. Give in there and you've a lot to do to come back.

Despite their popularity, the big sidecars have a growing problem, and that's money. They cost a great deal to maintain and each new development has to be matched to stay on equal terms. Prize money is not enough to give even the most successful drivers a profit and so the sacrifices are many and hard. It is the branch of grass track that demands the most dedication from those who take part.

Even so, new and younger partnerships continue to appear, though there is no school-boy class for three-wheelers. Perhaps this, too, may come and ensure the future of sidecars in much the same way that solo grass track can look forward to a supply of teenagers who became masters before they cease to be pupils.

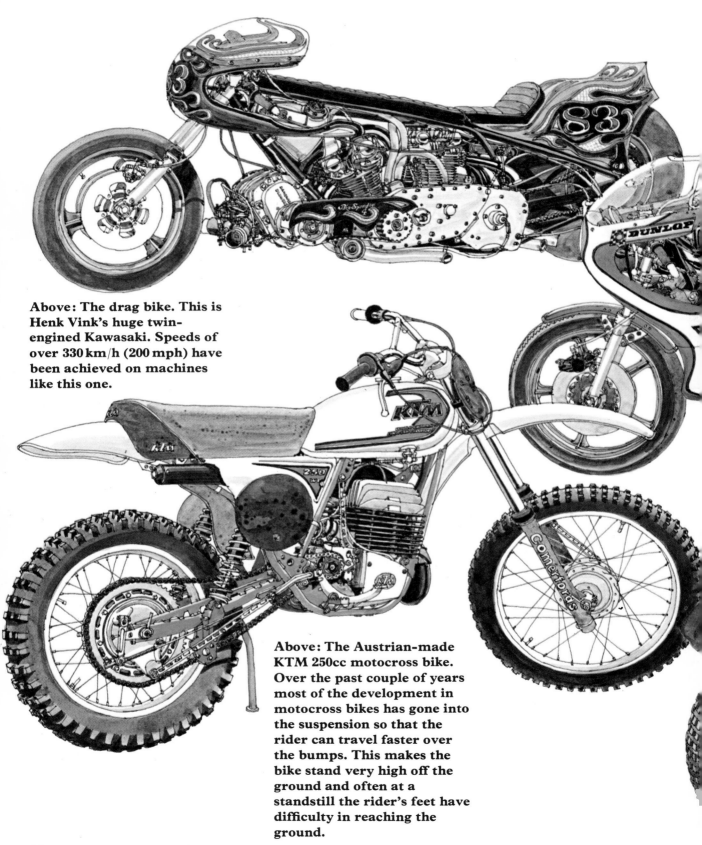

Above: The drag bike. This is Henk Vink's huge twin-engined Kawasaki. Speeds of over 330 km/h (200 mph) have been achieved on machines like this one.

Above: The Austrian-made KTM 250cc motocross bike. Over the past couple of years most of the development in motocross bikes has gone into the suspension so that the rider can travel faster over the bumps. This makes the bike stand very high off the ground and often at a standstill the rider's feet have difficulty in reaching the ground.

# The Machines

Left: Typical of the modern breed of Japanese road-racing bikes is this Kawasaki 250cc machine painted in the familiar Kawasaki green.
Above: The four-valve Jawa which is one of the most popular of speedway bikes.

Built in Spain, the Bultaco 350 trials bike has become one of the most successful trials machines.

# Trial Riding

The most exacting and skilful sport on two wheels is trials riding. This may seem a little odd to many who point out that the bikes used are small enough to pick up and speeds in the event rarely exceeds 10 mph. However, the trial is the ultimate test of machine control and if you can make the grade in trial riding, the chances are you will be able to shine in any branch of the sport.

A trial takes place usually in the most rugged inaccessible place you could imagine, and involves each rider taking a turn to complete a section. The idea is to complete this section losing the fewest marks. The penalties are: one mark for dabbing (touching the ground with one foot), two marks for touching twice, three marks for any more dabs and five for stopping completely. The rider with fewest marks over the many sections wins and in international competition, this can mean as few as a handful of points lost in the whole event.

Obstacles encountered in the woodlands vary from 45° muddy slopes and U-turns around saplings to traversing fast-running streams layered with slimy rocks. In televised events in arenas, the usual obstructions are a 50 gallon drum on its side, a batch of tractor tyres which have to be ridden in and out of, a builders' skip and a Volkswagen Beetle which has to be ridden over. Next time you come up to one in traffic, imagine how difficult it would be to ride over without putting your feet down.

Just like any sport, the key to trial riding is smoothness. With a small bike and the rider constantly standing on the pegs, smooth throttling is imperative: too little and the bike will stop, too much and the

**Right: Top rider Martin Lampkin negotiates a tricky part of the 1981 World Championship course.**

**Below: Rob Shepherd scales a tough hill.**

machine's acceleration will either tie the rider in knots, break the rear wheel's traction or both. Careful braking is needed, too, again to avoid the wheels stopping, which will usually mean instant rectification by a mark-losing touch of the ground.

Although heavy four-strokes were once the order of the day, today's machines are tiny two-strokes mostly with the accent on light weight and smooth power delivery. Very low gearing is needed not only to mount the steep obstacles, but also to enable the rider to let in the clutch and forget it even at speeds of as little as 1–2 mph.

Sidecar trials are very different in that with a stable three-wheeler there isn't such a need to touch down. However, a sidecar outfit is very unwieldy and needs almost telepathic communication between rider and passenger to make sure the whole plot doesn't tip over. Uphill, too, the passenger has to position his weight to make sure the rear driving wheel gets the traction it needs. Once that wheel starts to spin on a steep incline, the chances are that the whole plot will quickly slide back down to the bottom again.

For the competitor, trials riding is the most popular British bike sport, with more events taking place than any other two-wheeled competition throughout the year. For the spectator, however, trials just do not offer anyone but the most knowledgable enthusiast the sort of thrills and spills that

**Right: Obstacles encountered on a trial are likely to be anything from woodland to a rocky stream.**

Left: Oops-a-daisy! Away go
Southampton Viking Club
officials George Herbert (left)
and Les Barrow.

Above: Jack Mathews, three
times British Sidecar Trials
Champion. His passenger
tries desperately to stop the
outfit tipping right over.

Overleaf: Trial riding
normally takes place in the
most inaccessible places –
mountainsides are not
excluded!

usually come part and parcel of
motorcycle competition. In
spite of this, the very best riders
earn impressive money, though
the sport more often offers
trophies to the successful
participants.

For the younger competitor,
trials may seem to be lacking in
the glamour lavished upon
motocross and road racing but
it is the ideal learning ground
for any form of the sport. A
useful trials machine is not
expensive and one can practise
almost anywhere there is some
free rough ground. Success is
more dependent on the rider
than any other branch of the
sport and nothing can be of
more use than hours and hours
of practice learning the finer

points of machine control.

This can be put to good use
in road racing, motocross or
speedway, but it is also a great
boon in road riding where
many accidents are caused by
inexperienced riders being unable to retain control of their
machines in adverse situations.

You only have to ask Ulster-
man Sammy Miller who, after a
successful career on the race
tracks took up trials riding and
was largely responsible for
making it such a popular sport
today. The 11 times British and
twice world trials champion has
won almost 1000 events, more
than twice as many as anybody
else.

# Road Racing

Road racing is *the* motor cycle sport and embodies the glamour and excitement of the world's best riders competing at the limit for top honours. In the blue riband 500cc class, star riders like Barry Sheene, Kenny Roberts, Marco Lucchinelli and Randy Mamola vie for position with their 130 bhp, 270 lb machines racing at speeds of up to 180 mph one second and then scrabbling through corners with their knees grazing the ground, and the slick tyres on the bikes tenuously hanging on to the tarmac. With as much as 50° of lean, the racers sweep through the corners, making their riders heroes to the legions of fans who swarm to the European Grand Prix circuits throughout the summer to catch a glimpse of the high-speed action.

Even though the days are long since past when British machines headed the grand prix packs, Britain is still the hub of the bike-racing world as the many events attract thousands of racers all competing with one aim in mind — to win.

The Japanese industry produces most of the machines on our roads nowadays, and it is those manufacturers which produce the racers in the hopes of getting their brand name in headlines around the world. All of the "Big Four" — Honda, Kawasaki, Suzuki and Yamaha — are competing in 500cc racing, each trying to emulate the Italian manufacturer, MV-Agusta, which achieved 37 world championship titles between the 1950s and the early 1970s.

Today, the sport is ultra-professional with the top teams spending hundreds of thousands of pounds in their quest for success with

**Below: Toni Mang gets the maximum benefit from his Kawasaki's streamlined shape.**

massive research and development departments slaving to gain the slightest edge or to counter any development by a rival team.

Road racing was progressing at a steady pace in the 1930s but in 1939, when the Second World War was declared, things came to a temporary halt. At that time British riders such as Freddie Frith, Harold Daniel and Stanley Woods were among the acknowledged top men with British machines including Velocette, Norton and Excelsior the most prominent on the result sheets. But there were some radical changes in store soon after racing got under way again in 1947.

A major step came in 1949 when the world championships were introduced and run over a series of events throughout Europe. The main venues were the Isle of Man, where the legendary circuit has been in operation since 1911, the Assen circuit in Holland and Spa-Francorchamps in Belgium. Racing on all three

**Above: Times change, both in fashion and in racing, as this picture shows. John Surtees pushes off his MV-4 at the start of the Senior TT some 20 years ago at the Isle of Man.**

of these closed roads circuits was staged in the years before the war with the Isle of Man TT history going back to 1907. For the first four years of its existence a shorter course in the St Johns area of the island was used, and the move was made to the longer circuit when it was felt that the fastest lap of 85.5 km/h (53.14 mph) and the winning average of Charlie Collier on a Matchless at 81.46 km/h (50.63 mph) in 1910 was "too fast for the existing circuit".

The first year in the Mountain Circuit, where riders had to contend with rutted tracks in parts, the fastest lap was 80.62 km/h (50.11 mph), a far cry from today where several riders have cracked the 20 minute barrier for the circuit at an average of 181.93 km/h (113 mph).

**Bottom of page: Typical sidecar and solo action at the best-known circuits in Britain – left, Donington and right, Brands Hatch. In sidecar racing, weight distribution is all important, especially when cornering.**

Graham Noyce, former British world champion, shows his exceptional control in near horizontal position going round a fast right-hander.

Bottom of page: Two great rivals for the World Road Racing Championships. Barry Sheene, left, was world champion in 1976 and 1977, while Kenny Roberts, right, won the title in the following three years.

**Above: Looking back to 1956 at short circuit racing at its best in the Scarborough International with Surtees (33) and Bob McIntyre (46) on 500cc Norton single-cylinder machines.**

**Right: Three world champions: Kenny Roberts, just ahead of reigning 500cc titleholder Marco Lucchinelli and Britain's Barry Sheene.**

Because of the danger factor and because money rewards at the time were inadequate, the top riders decided to boycott the TT after the 1972 races and the event was stripped of its full world championship status in 1976. A special TT Formula championship was introduced in 1977, and with the money offered greatly increased the top riders are returning to the Island.

The introduction of the world championship brought increased interest from the Italian factories with Moto Guzzi, well in the picture before the war, claiming the 250cc title in the first year. Another Italian factory, Mondial, clinched the smallest 125cc championship but Velocette with Freddie Frith, AJS with Les Graham and Norton with Eric Oliver were successful in the 350cc, 500cc, and sidecar classes respectively.

But the British machine representation at the top was to be short-lived with Norton the last British solo machine to win a championship when Geoff Duke won the 350cc title in 1952, and the same factory taking the sidecar championship with Oliver the following year for the final time.

Although British machines were knocked from the top as Gilera and MV moved in to the solo classes, and the German BMW concern took over the sidecar section for a 20-year run that ended in 1975 when Klaus Enders took the title with a Konig powered outfit, British riders continued to be dominant. The first time a British rider failed to take a world championship was 1972 and a similar situation occurred in 1975 and 1978.

It was in 1961 that the Japanese broke into the grand prix scene and Honda, with Australian Tom Phillis and Britain's Mike Hailwood, were first to get to the top with triumphs in the 125cc and 250cc world championships.

In 1962 the 50cc world championship was introduced and this was snapped up by Suzuki with West German Ernst Degner aboard one of its incredible two-stroke midgets.

With the exception of MV which dominated the 500cc class, the Italian factories bowed out of the championships and the series developed into expensive almost bitter duels between rival Oriental teams.

Yamaha, with rider Phil Read, chalked up its first championship in 1964 with success in the 250cc class when it fielded four-cylinder two-stroke multis from Honda.

The MV stranglehold in the 500cc class was remarkable. It was first successful in 1956 with John Surtees as rider and had a champion on its books until 1974. For the last two years before it pulled out of racing the champion was Read with Italian Giacomo Agostini holding the crown for the seven years between 1966 and 1972. Others to gain the title for the factory were Hailwood and Gary Hocking.

The six class world championship pattern continued until 1976 when the Formula 750 series was granted full recognition by the Federation Internationale Motocycliste, which overlords all international motorcycle sport. This was, however, to have a short life, because in 1978 the FIM announced that from 1980 the 750cc class was to be dropped from the world series.

In pruning the championships further, the 350cc class was to be dropped from the end of the 1982 season.

When road racing started, and in the early days of the championships, many of the circuits were closed roads circuits, but in recent years, with growing concern for safety as speeds soar, there has been a move to purpose-built circuits like our own Brands Hatch and Silverstone.

The fastest grand prix circuit was Francorchamps with top speeds reaching 290 km/h (180 mph) and with lap speeds in the region of 225 km/h (140 mph) for the 500cc machines. For safety and ease of organisation this 12.87 kilometres (8 miles) closed roads circuit was modified and shortened to just over 4.8 kilometres (3 miles) for the 1979 grand prix.

In recent years, the Americans have steadily become involved in grand prix racing with Steve Baker taking his works' Yamaha to the 1977 Formula 750 title and Pat Hennen becoming the first American to win a 500cc grand prix in the same year.

These two were both overshadowed by Kenny Roberts who took the title in his first attempt in 1978 and repeated this in the following two years. Since 1974, when MV took its last 500 title with its four-stroke racer, two-stroke machines have dominated the 500 class with first Suzuki and then Yamaha.

The two-strokes' light weight and incredible

Far left: Former world champion Kenny Roberts in the 1981
Finnish Grand Prix.
Centre left: Toni Mang, the reigning world 250cc and 350cc
champion, on the way to another victory.
Bottom left: Taylor and Johansson, former world champions,
show that the partner in the sidecar must work just as hard as
the rider.
Above: Toni Mang carries the distinctive No 1, signifying his
championship rank.

power outputs have given them the edge and not even a multi-million pound onslaught by Honda with their NR500 in 1980 and 1981 could put the once-dominant four-stroke back on top. In the end, Honda had to resort to a two-stroke itself for 1982, something it didn't want to do because most of its road-bike range has been built solidly round the four-stroke-engine design.

Two stroke road bikes have become increasingly rare because of their thirst and polluting exhausts and it only remains to be seen whether the governing body of the sport decides to outlaw the "strokers" on the tracks, so that once again the racers will be identifiable with the roadsters that you can buy in your local showroom . . . just as it used to be.

**Above:** Mike Hailwood, seen here on a 750cc Yamaha, staged a sensational comeback at the 1978 Isle of Man TT races on an Italian Ducati to increase his world championship tally to ten.
**Right:** Kenny Roberts was the first American to win the 500cc world championship. Note the slick front tyre on Kenny's Yamaha in this excellent action shot, which emphasises the "angle of lean" possible on modern racing machines.

Above: Dave Taylor, known as the "Wheelie King", has completed an entire circuit of the 59 km (37 miles) TT course in the Isle of Man on the back wheel of his bike. Below and right: The Imps display team which is made up of boys between the ages of 8 and 16 years.

# Stuntmen

Although there have always been people around performing stunts on motorcycles, like police and army display teams and wall-of-death riders, it has only been in recent years that individual stuntmen have come to the fore, and that is largely through the efforts of American superstar Evel Knievel. Many riders around the world have now equalled or bettered his famous motorcycle jumps, but it was his showmanship which made him world famous, drawing thousands of people wherever he performed, with his sequined stars-and-stripes outfit and powerful Harley-Davidson motorcycle.

Most riders use lighter motocross-style bikes, but Evel sticks to his heavy Harley. In fact, it is because he uses such a big bike that he has been so badly injured in the past. In famous leaps at Caesar's Palace, Las Vegas, and Wembley, he has tumbled and his heavy bike has landed on top of him. A 250 lb motocrosser is one thing, but 500 lb of Harley is something else!

Evel's most famous stunt was his attempt at

**Below: Eddie Kidd's star turn is a hair-raising leap over a line of double-decker buses.**

crossing the Snake River canyon on a rocket-powered bike, a stunt which nobody believed he would even attempt. However, his rocket bike duly took off, rose several hundred feet and parachuted gently down to the ground far below. It was never going to work, but Mr Showmanship had the world's TV and press there just in case it did . . .

Britain's own Eddie Kidd has set several world records for jumping. On one stunt he bridged a collapsed 80 ft viaduct without a launching ramp during filming a story based loosely on his life, *Riding High*. Eddie has easily outjumped all of Knievel's records and displays an uncanny control of his motorcycle just like the best moto cross riders.

Another Briton, Dave Taylor, started a trend for pulling "wheelies", where the bike is brought on to its rear wheel only, at every opportune moment, usually showing his talents at major race meetings around Europe between the main events.

Dave has made full "wheelie" laps of most GP circuits and has even lapped the full 37-mile TT course on the back wheel of his trail bike. Dave is very actively involved in young-rider training and road safety, and uses his skills showing youngsters how important proper control is for all situations.

Next on the "wheelie" scene was American Doug Domokos, who was out to prove that if someone could thrill crowds with a 500cc trail bike, he would leave them open mouthed with his Kawasaki Z1300, almost 700 lb of heavyweight, six-cylinder tourer. Not content with just elevating the front wheel, he lifted it so far that the number plate at the rear scraped the ground!

Another Z1300 rider was soon joining the action and proving that the sky is the limit when bike stunts are the order of the day. Finnish rider Arto "Archie" Nyquist warms up by doing almost vertical wheelies on a trail bike before pulling wheelies on his Z1300 . . . sitting backwards! He is also able to accelerate the bike flat out while facing the rear and has even been known to jump the bike that way, too. He then dons his wooden clogs and gets the bike up to 100 mph or so, and then slips back on the seat before stepping off the rear of the bike and skiing along in a waft of smoke from his smouldering footwear as the bike slows down.

In a recent tour of Britain, he performed most of his repertoire with his left leg in plaster. As they say, you don't have to be mad to do these stunts, but it helps.

**Left: Ace stuntman Eddie Kidd does not need bridges to cross railway lines. This spectacular leap spanned 145 feet.**

**Below: Kidd makes his famous 80 foot jump over Devil's Leap in a scene from the film *Very Heavy Metal*.**

# Superbikes

The age of the "Superbike" started in 1969, an era which was firmly based around the arrival of the first Japanese multi-cylinder machine, the Honda 750 Four. In the preceding years, a 500cc twin was regarded as a large machine and the roads were populated by all manner of British bikes which were basically updated variants on machines first produced after the Second World War. Although the British bike industry was already in a sad state of decline, there was little else to buy unless you could afford the much more expensive American and German machines.

When the mighty Honda arrived, the whole attitude to large machines had to change. In one stroke, the performance parameters of big bikes shot up as the Honda reached a top speed of more than 120 mph, yet was still able to return better than 40 mpg given a gentle right wrist.

Four-cylinder, across-the-frame engines were not new (the Italian race manufacturers had been using them since the 1950s) but the Hondas was so smooth and responsive, quiet and refined, that it caused bike journalists something of a headache trying to describe the bike without resorting to cliché terms like "turbine-like smoothness" and "akin to the sound of a sewing machine".

In spite of the praise lavished on the bike, few realised that in 10 short years, bikes like the Honda would be the norm rather than the exception. Kawasaki soon announced their 903cc Z900, which for many years was to lead the field with its blistering yet usable performance. Alongside the Z900, Kawasaki was building a reputation with its lightweight two-strokes with race-track acceleration, particularly their 500cc H1 which would pull "wheelies" at inopportune moments and which cornered with marked reluctance because of a chassis that wasn't as well developed as it might have been. The larger 750cc two-stroke Kawasaki was a little less temperamental and ultimately a little faster, but it was easily outclassed by the Z900 which was so much easier to ride fast and didn't drink gallons of fuel while so doing.

Running the two different types of bike, Kawasaki soon found that the future lay with the four-stroke multi and soon all the big four Japanese manufacturers were using the blueprint of the four-stroke, four-cylinder engine for a whole range of bikes from as little as 350cc (used by Honda for the European version of the CB400) to 1100cc like the Yamaha XS1100 and the Suzuki GS1100. Indeed, this now classic engine configuration was being dubbed UJM or Universal Japanese Multi, and being looked upon in the same mundane light as the pushrod-valve in-line twin during the 1950s and 1960s.

Honda, which produces more internal-combustion engines than anyone else in the world, was soon veering away from the UJM concept for some of its models. Its 1000cc Gold Wing tourer featured a flat-four motor with water cooling which helped make it the quietest of the large multis. With shaft drive and bags of pulling power, the Gold Wing was ideal for long distances and in America especially it found a ready market.

Honda's next variation on the multi theme was as impractical and stunning as the Gold Wing was useful and understated, and merely proved a point that the Honda development department, given a free hand, could still turn a few heads. The CBX featured a six-cylinder motor across the frame, twin overhead camshafts and four valves to a cylinder. With such complexities as hollow camshafts for light weight, the 1047cc bike produced 105 bhp and had a top speed of close to 140 mph. More sensibly, a 95 bhp four-cylinder Honda, the B900, came on the market not long after and had virtually the same performance as its more exotic stablemate. In the meantime, Kawasaki got its six-cylinder model ready and displayed to the world their Z1300 which boasted 120 bhp, making it the most powerful production motorcycle offered.

The touring Kawasaki Z1300 marked an important turning point in the age of the superbike. In the three years since its announcement, the Z1300 has remained the largest of the Japanese multis with the trend turning

towards making the middle-size fours more efficient. Kawasaki's own GP550 was a case in point, as the 1982 model had virtually the same performance to offer as the pioneering Z900 of 10 years before. Lighter bikes with more

**Above: Honda believe that this bike will be so attractive to thieves that they have fitted a special anti-theft device as standard equipment. This VF750S Sports is the world's first water-cooled V4 motorcycle.**

efficient and therefore more powerful engines are the norm now, with the recent emergence of the turbocharger being the focal point in this new swing in technology.

Basically, a turbocharger is a rotor which sits in the exhaust system and spins at speeds of up to 150,000 rpm as the exhaust gases speed past. This rotor is connected to another rotor in the inlet stream which in turn forces the mixture into the engine and so increasing performance.

The beauty of the system is that the extra power is free in that it is using energy in the exhaust system which would normally be lost. Its disadvantage is that if the extra boost of energy is not properly controlled, it can turn an expensive engine into so much scrap metal. Honda again led the way with their turbocharged CX500 which made use of all sorts of microprocessors and advanced electronics to monitor the system, but they were quickly followed by Yamaha with a turbo 650-four, Suzuki with its turbo 650-four and Kawasaki which, just to continue a quest for ultimate performance, announced a prototype turbo 750-four. Each had performance well in line with normally aspirated 1000s and 1100s.

Although superbikes are not purely the domain of the Japanese, that country's industry is the only one which can afford the technology to quench the market's thirst for better and faster bikes. Italy, which has fairly strict import controls on Japanese imports, has a healthy superbike industry, but it would be the first to admit that it cannot hope to compete on equal terms. Instead it concentrates on simple lighter bikes which are renowned for their handling and road-holding. BMW has been the only German company producing large bikes for many years, and its flat-twin models have a reputation for being outstanding tourers with economical performance and great comfort.

The age of the superbike has been one of increasing size and performance, but since the fuel crises, manufacturers are becoming increasingly aware of the need to preserve precious fuels. So money is being spent on making bikes lighter and more efficient. But they won't be getting any slower.

**Below: Power on two wheels from Suzuki's four-cylinder 1100cc "Beast".**

**Above: The CX500 T-C Turbo from Honda
has a digital computer controlling its fuel
injection system. The turbo-charger gives the
500cc bike spectacular power.**

# Speedway

## 50 Glorious years

Speedway celebrated its Golden Jubilee in Britain in September 1978 and fittingly the world championship was decided at the famous Wembley stadium, London before 90,000 fans.

After a gripping championship, the title was won by Denmark's Ole Olsen. His five races, spread throughout a twenty heat programme, took just over five minutes to run, but winning the coveted crown can earn the rider around £100,000 in the following year.

Speedway, it is generally agreed, came to England in 1928 when the new art of "broadsliding" round the corners was first demonstrated by pioneer Australian riders.

The sport caught on in a big way; leagues were set up and competitors from the United States of America and Australia came over to ride for English teams. The world championship, the sport's premier event, was introduced in 1936 at Wembley. The first world champion was an Australian, Lionel Van Praag, who won after a run-off with England's Eric Langton.

The world championship has been held every year since 1936, apart from during the war

**Above: Dave Jessup, the former schoolboy grass track champion, is one of England's leading speedway riders.**

years. It was in the first post-war final in 1949 that England had its first world champion, Tommy Price, who was unbeaten in his five races.

Speedway is the 'odd ball' in motorcycle sport. Races are held on oval shale circuits up to about 400 metres round, and riders negotiate four laps on purpose-built machines which have *no brakes* and *no gears!* The bikes have 500cc four-stroke, single-cylinder engines

72

built into a flexible "diamond" frame. In the pioneer days several firms produced speedway machines, like Douglas and Rudge. As the sport became more professional and more competitive, one great British engine was to come to the fore. This was the JAP motor built by J.A. Prestwich. Examples of this amazing engine dominated the sport for 35 years. This bike produced the right kind of power needed for speedway. The engine has to be powerful from low revs so that riders can get out of the gate quickly, but also be quick enough down the straights.

The domination of this English engine was broken by the Czechoslovakian firm of Jawa. It was very much an updated version of the JAP, pioneered in world speedway by New Zealander Barry Briggs, winner of four world titles. Then came the reintro-

duction of four-valve engines into the sport by another British firm, Weslake. A lot of early development work on the Weslake engine was completed by John Louis, the England and Ipswich rider, in 1974.

The Weslake has already made history because it powered the first Englishman to a world championship since the late Peter Craven won in 1962. It was this engine which gave Belle Vue's Peter Collins his world championship title in 1976 in Poland. Another Englishman, Malcolm Simmons of Poole, came second, on another Weslake.

The Czech Jawa company countered the superiority of the Weslake four-valve machine, with the introduction of their own four-valve engine – and indeed, it was this motor which powered Ole Olsen to success in the world championship at Wembley in 1978, and Ivan

**Above: The lightweight flexible frame allows the rider to perform spectacular broadsliding manoeuvres.**

Mauger in 1977 and 1979.

Nowadays a speedway rider's life is a hectic one. England has undisputedly the best league system in the world and all but a handful of the world's top stars ride in Britain for British teams. These top riders ride five, six or even seven times a week, travelling between West Germany, Sweden, Czechoslovakia, Poland all through the summer.

England, supreme for many years in world team events because of its strength in depth, has produced very few individual world champions. We can only look to Price in 1949, Craven in 1955 and 1962, Collins in 1976 and Michael Lee in 1980. We must not forget, however, that a Welsh-

73

man, Freddie Williams, won in 1950 and 1953. The countries supreme in the world championship have been Sweden and New Zealand.

Sweden produced one of the greatest riders of all, Ove Fundin, who became a legend in his own lifetime, winning the title five times in 1956, 1960, 1961, 1963 and 1967 after finishing last in his first world final appearance in 1954.

New Zealand, through Ronnie Moore, Barry Briggs and Ivan Mauger also have a tremendous record in the world finals. Moore was the first of the world championship New Zealanders to come over to England, joining Wimbledon. Moore, one of the best stylists that the sport has ever seen, won championships in 1954 and 1959. A youngster who idolised Moore came over from New Zealand to join Wimbledon. That was Barry Briggs

who, in the number of titles he won, outshone his hero. He won in 1957, 1958, 1964 and 1966. Then came the most famous New Zealanders of all – Ivan Mauger. He came over to England first of all as a teenager, failed to make the top grade and returned home. Then he made a second attempt, came back and went right to the top! If at first you don't succeed.... To Mauger must go credit for making speedway professional in its outlook and giving it respectability in the eyes of the sporting world. His record six titles came in 1968, 1969, 1970, 1972 and 1977.

Those are just a few of the famous names that have been cheered by millions of fans over the years. Seen under floodlights, speedway is a great spectacle, with the competitors riding shoulder to shoulder, and leathers gleaming. For

**Above: The tapes go up and four riders rev up in a typical speedway start. The instant battle is on for supremacy at the very first bend.**

**Left: Typical speedway action from Doug Wyer, Mike Lee, Scott Autrey and Phil Collins, in an exciting and dramatic fight for position.**

**Right: Ivan Mauger, the mightiest New Zealander of all, is one of speedway's most popular superstars.**

**Above: Reigning world speedway champion Bruce Penhall of the US shows that speedway is no sport for worrying about dirtying your bike!**

**Left: Ronnie Moore, the first of the World Champions from New Zealand.**

sheer excitement speedway takes some beating!

Speedway is Britain's second largest spectator sport, second only to football, and is seen every night of the week somewhere in the country.

# Index
The figures in italics refer to illustrations